This book is a very special gift...

For: _____

From: _____

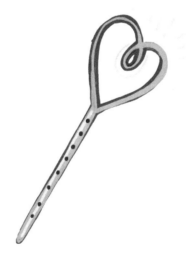

First Printing, 2018
ISBN-13: 978-1-7322230-0-4

Loved + Wanted PRESS
PO Box 907
Lyons, CO 80540

LovedandWanted.com

This book is lovingly dedicated to birthmothers, their children and adoptive families everywhere (especially Marc and Vivienne), with deepest, heartfelt admiration and gratitude for Harmony and Bridget.

And to Jane...our friend, our champion, and the mother of all mentors. Thank you for believing in us!

- AH, MHH

My hope is always for people to practice love; to be aware of how love is not always perfect, but forgives and embraces us right where we are.

Families, in all shapes and sizes, are a big, beautiful gift and should be celebrated for everything that they are.

-DD

You were the one who
gave birth to me

Then made a big decision
that set me free.

I have a body that came from you
And the life I have because you knew...

...You could not give
all you wished for me.

So, through adoption
it was agreed I'd be

Raised with enough
and parented well

Surrounded by love
and a safe place to dwell.

You wanted for me to grow up
healthy and strong

With all that I needed
to be cared for my entire lifelong.

This choice was not easy
or made without loss,

But no one gets through life
without hurdles to cross.

So, in those times
when I am lonely or sad

Or something feels missing
and my day has gone bad,

I will take a sweet, deep breath
and place my hand over my heart

Feeling you close,
of me you are part.

When moments come
where I wonder about you,

And I have a question
with no clear answer or clue...

I will feel your pure spirit
woven together with mine.

Your presence a comfort;
your courage my guide.

I will know you are with me celebrating all of my firsts,

And wanting for me to feel and heal all of my hurts.

first bike

When I perform in front
of an audience on stage

Or flip through the family album
page by page,

Or on birthdays
with flaming candles aglow

and at holiday-time
making angels in snow,

I will hear you whispering
in my hopeful ear...

You are loved.

You are wanted.

My darling,

my dear.

I will imagine you waving
your bright, twinkling wand

Making magic at night
blessing our rare,
sacred bond.

Belonging in my family
and
believing in you

Helps my world make sense
so my dreams can come true.

For as time unfolds
and I move through each year,

I become wiser;
your existence more clear.

I will see you.
I will feel you.
I will know you

As not some
mysterious who

Or a curious person
I never knew.

With purpose and promise,
you delivered and flew.

From your sacrifice
and with strength and support,
I grew.

You are mine,
and I am yours.

We belong to each other
and each to another...

My beautiful, brave and beloved
Fairy Birthmother.

You are so
loved and wanted
in this world.

CPSIA information can be obtained
at www.ICGtesting.com
Printed in the USA
LVHW072059140422
716230LV00009B/310